MARINE MAMMALS OF ALASKA
A FIELD GUIDE FOR CHILDREN

*The **I Saw It!** Series #2: Field Guides, Journals, and Coloring Books for Children*

by

Barbara L. Brovelli-Moon *Ms Barb*

Artwork by Kimberly A. Sherry

Junior Naturalist:_____   **Date:**_____

Ocean Otter PUBLISHING

ANCHORAGE, ALASKA

Brovelli-Moon, Barbara (Illustrator, Kim Sherry)

Marine Mammals of Alaska: A Field Guide for Children
The I Saw It! Series #2: Field Guides, Journals, and Coloring Books for Children

ISBN: 978-0-9962559-3-6

Published by OceanOtter Publishing

Designed by Phillip Gessert

Edited by Norma Neill and Amy Frackman

Printed in the United States of America

10 9 8 7 6 5 4 3 2 1

Contact the author at oceanotterpublishing@gmail.com or www.oceanotterpublishing.com

See more of Kim Sherry's art work at www.kimsherrygallery.com

Table of Contents
And Checklist of Sightings

In Memoriam

Allan A. Trefry, mentor and friend. Thank you for sharing your love of music, *The Life of Pi*, and for teaching me to live life fully. You are missed by so many.

Vince Correa, who left Kara and Eric far too soon. You are deeply missed.

James Verhaeghe II, an amazing student who taught us all so much.

Madeline and Millie, my canine companions, who saw so many of Alaska's mammals with me.

Acknowledgements

Thanks, Mike Kemmer, for the idea. Kim Sherry, the drawings are exactly what I wanted. Amy Frackman, thanks for ongoing tech help, reading, and rounding up sixth graders to edit—you're amazing. Norma Neill and Linda Wichman, thanks for the painstaking, last-minute editing. Sakura Likar, Sandy Pendergast, Carol Dickason, Linda Hawkins, and Maureen Jones, thanks for reading and making suggestions. Brayden and Brennen Battle of Battleboys' Graphics, thank you for your terrific coloring , and Laila Moore, you are a great artist! Isabel Jones, Maya and Sophie Sherry, and McNeeley and Maudie Mae Olson, you are great kid editors! The glossary search kids at Northern Lights ABC School in Anchorage, Alaska—Yael, Sonja, Losi, Zayn, Sharon, Maisha, Shreya, Ashlieyh, Ashley, Riley, Ariana, and Amaret—you did great work. Jeanette Troup, Kelly Fisher, and Jim Barr, thanks for your varied ideas. Gene Dickason, thanks for the use of some of your great photographs. And Greg, what a ride we decided to take. Thanks for being at my side.

Special thanks to the Alaska Department of Fish and Game for allowing me to use information from your website, including the maps showing where the mammals live. Additionally, special thanks to Marcella Asicksik, Language Project Coordinator at the Alaska Native Heritage Center, who provided many of the Native name translations. Your assistance is greatly appreciated.

Cover photograph by Pilot Gene Dickason

Back cover drawing colored by Grandson Brennen Battle

Introduction

Hello, and welcome to the world of mammals. What is a mammal, you ask? A mammal is an animal who *has a backbone, lungs to breathe air, grows hair or fur on its body*, and *gives birth to live babies who drink milk from their mother*.

This book, *Marine Mammals of Alaska*, is . . .

. . . a field guide in which twenty marine mammals tell their own stories. You will learn where they live, what they eat, how they act, and so much more.

. . . a journal that gives you a place to write your own story about seeing these mammals. Where were you? Who was with you? What happened? Keep a record of your experiences as you see these amazing creatures.

. . . a coloring book for you to color the images of each mammal. Follow the descriptions given to color them accurately, or color them pink, green, orange, or purple. This is your book to use as you choose.

The book also includes a checklist to record when you have seen one of the mammals, names for the mammals in some of the Alaska Native languages, an explanation of the difference between common and scientific names, a chart of names for the males, females, offspring, and groups of a species, a glossary, and other hidden surprises! And, if you want to meet the land mammals mentioned in this book, pick up a copy of *Land Mammals of Alaska for Children* and read their stories, too.

Enjoy getting to know the amazing marine mammals of Alaska!

Why Do We All Have Three Names?

Hi. Bella Polar Bear here. Every mammal in this book has three names listed at the top of their story page. Why do we have three names? Let me explain by telling you about my names, which are . . .

Polar Bear
Mooksgm'ol in Sm'algayx • *Ursus maritimus*

The first name listed is my common or popular name used by English-speaking people. That name is **Polar Bear**. The second name listed is the common or popular name in one of the more than twenty Alaska Native languages. I am known as **Mooksgm'ol** in the Sm'algayx language. My name is capitalized in this Native language, but sometimes Native names are not capitalized. All the mammals in this book have an English common name along with a name from one of the many Native languages.

The third name listed is my scientific name, ***Ursus maritimus***. Everything living on our planet has a scientific name created by scientists. These complicated names are used to be absolutely positive about the exact identity of the life form being discussed or studied. Seven classifications, or divisions, make up my long scientific name:

Kingdom, **Phylum**, **Class**, **Order**, **Family**, **Genus**, and **Species**

("**K**ids **P**refer **C**andy **O**ver **F**resh **G**reen **S**alad" will help you remember!)

Kingdom is the largest classification, and each division after that becomes more and more specific. My scientific name is below, with a few of the characteristics that describe each classification.

Classification	Name	Characteristics
Kingdom	Animalia	Animal
Phylum	Chordata	Vertebrate (an animal with a backbone)
Class	Mammalian	Mammal
Order	Carnivora	Meat-eater
Family	Ursidae	All bears
Genus	*Ursus*	Black, brown, polar, sun, and sloth bears
Species	*maritimus*	Polar or sea bear

Everyone's scientific name is based on a Latin or Greek root. "Animalia" comes from the Latin root "animale," and "mammalian" comes from the Latin root "mammalis." Many English words come from these same roots, like animal and mammal. Scientific names are so long, scientists use only the last two categories, genus and species, when they talk about me or any other life form. So in this book, the third name, written in Latin, is my genus and species. Now you know!

Common Marine Mammal Families

Bear	Otter	Eared Seal	True Seal (Earless)	Walrus	Baleen Whales	Toothed Whales		
polar	sea	fur	bearded	walrus	blue			
		sea lion	harbor		bowhead	**Dolphins**	**Porpoises**	**Whales**
			ringed		fin	dolphins	Dall's	beluga
					gray	killer whale	harbor	sperm
					humpback			
					menke			

Male, Female, Baby, and Group Names

Mammal	Male	Female	Baby	Group
polar bear	boar	sow	cub	aurora, pack
seals	bull	cow	pup, calf	pod, colony
Steller sea lion	bull	cow	pup, calf	pod, bob, herd
dolphin, porpoise, walrus, whale	bull	cow	calf	pod, herd

Extra Field Notes:_____

Polar Bear

Mooksgm'ol in Sm'algayx • Ursus maritimus

Hello from the pack ice! I'm Bella Polar Bear, your local sea bear. It's October, and I've been out on the ice eating seals for months. Now I'm on my way to the rocky, barren coast to find a snow bank where I'll build my igloo-like den. I make a den only when I'm having cubs, which is every two or three years. Otherwise, my kind stays active throughout the year. But soon, in December or January, I'll give birth to my cubs, probably twins, and stay with them in our safe, warm den until late March when they are big enough to trek, or roam, with me.

With them, I limit my wanderings. When I'm alone, though, I travel about six hundred miles a year following the edge of the ice, always searching for my favorite food, Sakura Ringed Seal. I grab her while she's sleeping on the ice, or, when she's swimming under the ice, I wait by her breathing hole to snatch her when she comes up for air. I even dig her pups out of their lairs, or dens, in snow caves on the ice. I am an aggressive, dangerous bear, closely related to Brayden and Brennan, the brown bears.

We all lived together millions of years ago, but over time, we separated. I ended up living here, in the far north, along the cold Arctic waters and ice pack. Since then, my body has had to make adaptations (ad-ap-TAY-shuns), or serious changes, in order to survive. Instead of a brown coat like my cousins, my thick, water-repellant fur slowly changed to white to allow me to blend in with the white snow and ice. Heavy, warm fur grew on the bottoms of my huge, partially webbed feet to protect them on the frozen ground. And I developed a four-inch layer of blubber under my thick, black skin to insulate (IN-suh-layt) me from the frigid temperatures. Even my body shape changed, becoming wedge-like to make swimming easier. Notice how my small head blends into my long neck then flows to my narrow shoulders? With this shape I slice right through the water, paddling as fast as six miles per hour. That's fast for a bear!

Now, don't try to swim with me, but see if you can find me. Look close to shore or out on the ice. Wave if I'm there!

My Facts

SIZE:
Boar: body, 8–9 feet long; 4–5.5 feet tall at shoulder; weight, up to 1,400 pounds
Sow: body, 5–6 feet long; 3–4 feet tall at shoulder; weight, up to 700 pounds

COLOR:
Body: white with yellowish tinge due to oil-rich diet of seals
Skin, eyes, nose, lips: black

FOOD:
Mainly carnivorous: seals (prefers ringed seals), whale and walrus carcasses, small mammals, bird eggs, some vegetation

DANGERS:
Male polar bears, transient killer whales, Alaska Native hunters

YEARS I LIVE:
25–30 years

Did You See Me? Tell Your Story! _____

_____

_____

DID YOU KNOW? The only people allowed to hunt for me are Alaska Natives. I am an important part of subsistence living for some Native people. They use my meat and blubber for food, and my fur for blankets and clothing.

Pacific White-Sided Dolphin

k'aan in Tlingit • Lagenorhynchus obliquidens

Have you ever been to Sea World or another marine park in the Lower 48? Did you watch the dolphins leap and flip for their trainers? Well, that's what I do here in Alaska's waters all on my own. Hi, I'm Donovan Dolphin, or "Lag" because of my Latin name. I'm having the best time flying high into the air, twisting and flipping. I'm easy to spot if you watch for my short, dark beak, or nose, and my dark, stocky body. My belly is white, and I have striking, light-colored stripes running the length of my body on both sides.

I'll be bounding out of the water or bow-riding next to a fast boat. And when I race a boat, I'm often with Polly Porpoise. People frequently confuse us when we are together, so remember that I leap and flip out of the water and Polly doesn't. Her body shape is similar to mine, and so is her coloring, but she is larger and heavier than I am. My head and dorsal fin are larger than hers, though, and my fin is quite distinctive. It has an obvious, backward-curving hook, like an old-fashioned sickle (SICK-el) farmers used in their fields long ago. The front part of my fin is dark, and the back is a light gray. And you won't see just one fin slicing through the water. My kind is very social, so we travel and hunt in pods, or groups, that include bulls, cows, and pups, as well as Dall's porpoises and friendly baleen whales.

Our herds may be several thousand in number, but our feeding pods include only about ten of us. We feed early in the morning or late in the afternoon, and members of the pod work together to find food. We search deep areas of the ocean, the continental shelf, and the shallow waters in bays and fjords (FEE-ords). Sometimes, near the surface, we join seagulls feeding on "bait balls," which are schools of small "bait" fish, like anchovies (AN-cho-vees). These little fish clump together in a big mass and swim in a circle near the surface of the water. My feeding pod will dive under the seagulls, circle the ball of fish, and close in for an easy meal.

But the best part of my day is when I am leaping and jumping, so be sure to call to me if you see me somersaulting through the air!

My Facts

SIZE:
Bull: body, 7–9 feet long; weight, 300–400 pounds
Cow: body, 5–6 feet long; weight, 175–225 pounds
COLOR:
Back, sides: dark grayish-green
Sides: light gray stripe
Belly: white
FOOD:
Carnivorous: squid and fish, including capelin, saury, anchovy, hake
DANGERS:
Transient killer whales, fishing nets and lines, pollution, ship strikes
YEARS I LIVE:
40–45 years

Did You See Me? Tell Your Story! _____

_____

_____

_____

DID YOU KNOW? Dolphins are actually small whales with a single blowhole, or nostril, for breathing. Our spectacular leaps and surface skimming serve the same purpose as breaching does for whales: signaling others, herding small fish, or just having fun.

Sea Otter

Arhnaq in Sugpiaq • Enhydra lutris kenyoni

Hi! I'm Olivia Otter, resting close to shore with my pup, Oleg. He's almost a year old and will soon leave to live on his own. We just shared a yummy lunch of clams, and now we are going to groom ourselves.

I eat over twenty pounds of food every day, and I use my chest as a dinner table. I dive down as far as two hundred fifty feet to the rocky ocean bottom, grab a clam, abalone (ab-uh-LOH-nee), sea urchin, or other shellfish and bring it to the surface. Then I float on my back and pull out the small rock I carry in a secret pouch in my armpit. I put the rock on my chest, hold the hard-shelled food in my short, finger-like front toes, and whack! I crash the hard shell down on the rock to crack it open. My strong teeth crunch away the rest of the shell to expose the soft, delicious meat inside. I use the rock as a tool, which makes me one of very few animals who know how to use tools.

But cracking and eating food on my chest creates a serious problem. If I want to survive in this icy water, I must keep my fur completely clean. You see, I don't have a layer of blubber like other marine mammals. Instead, I have an amazing fur coat with long, waterproof guard hairs that protect my incredibly thick underfur. This inch-long undercoat is the densest hair coat of any mammal on Earth, with almost one million hairs per square inch. (You have about one hundred thousand hairs on your whole head!) Air is trapped in this fluffy, heavy coat and held close to my body to be warmed. The warmed air insulates (IN-suh-layts) me against the frigid water temperatures, keeping me four times warmer than blubber would. But if my fur collects any oil, salt crystals, or food, it packs down and air won't collect. If this happens, my skin becomes wet and cold, and I could freeze to death. So, unless I am eating or sleeping, I'll be cleaning my fur.

To find me when I'm sleeping, look for me bobbing in the water on my back, or wrapped in an anchored stipe, or branch, in the kelp beds with some of my family. I'll be close to shore, so wave if you see me!

My Facts

SIZE:
Boar: body, 30–45 inches long; tail, 9–15 inches long; weight, 50–100 pounds
Sow: slightly smaller than boar

COLOR:
Outer guard hairs: dark brown or black with silver tips giving frosted appearance
Underfur: brown to black
Head: grayish

FOOD:
Carnivorous: clams, crab, sea urchins, pinto abalones, mussels, octopi, fish

DANGERS:
Transient killer whales, oil spills, fishing nets and lines, pollution, Alaska Native hunters, bald eagles (pups)

YEARS I LIVE:
Bull: 15–20 years
Sow: longer than bull

Did You See Me? Tell Your Story! _____

_____

_____

_____

DID YOU KNOW? In the early 1900s, my kind was hunted almost to extinction for our unique fur. Now, our population is stable, and ninety percent of us live in Alaska's waters. I was voted the cutest mammal in Alaska. Do you agree?

Dall's Porpoise

k'aang in Haida • Phocoenoides dalli

Wow! Do I love zooming in this great big ocean! I'm Polly Porpoise, the fastest mammal on Earth. I swim up to thirty-five miles per hour, making it impossible for predators to catch me. I go so fast that when I break the surface of the water, I create a huge, curved splash, or "rooster tail," off my head and dorsal fin. No one else creates this kind of water curl when they skim the surface.

I have to come to the surface in order to breathe through the blowhole, or nostril, on top of my head. You see, all porpoises and dolphins are actually small, toothed cetaceans (si-TAY-shen), or whales, and I breathe just like my larger relatives. But please, don't confuse me with my most dangerous relative, Warrick Killer Whale. Some people think we are the same creature because we both have shiny, jet-black bodies with white bellies and sides. He is much larger than I am, and his tall, all-black dorsal fin stands straight up out of the water. My fin is a small triangle with black on the tip and edges only. My body is stocky and muscular, but not nearly as round as Warrick's. I'm more like a chubby torpedo (tor-PEE-doh), tapering to my blunt head and in back to my strong tail.

There is a huge mass of muscles at the end of my tail stock that make a noticeable hump, too. These muscles help me move my tail up and down quickly and strongly when I swim, which is part of the reason I'm such a speedster. And I love speeding beside boats and ships, bow-riding in front of them, shooting through their wakes, and darting from one side to the other. I jump out of the water a little, but I don't do leaps and flips like Donovan Dolphin. I race boats, though, for as long as half an hour, whether we are in deep, open water or in narrow, inland passages.

And you won't see me by myself, as I have lots of friends and relatives. Dolphins, porpoises, and friendly whales all hang out with me. Usually I'm with a group of three to twenty, but sometimes hundreds of us will gather if we find a large school of fish to share. So watch for a crowd, and the speedy one chasing a boat. That's me!

My Facts

SIZE:
Bull: body, 6–7 feet long; weight, 300–450 pounds
Cow: slightly smaller than bull
COLOR:
Body: shiny, jet-black
Sides, belly: large white patches
Dorsal fin: black with wide white stripe
FOOD:
Carnivorous: squid (preferred), hake, herring, saury, mackerel, bottom fish
DANGERS:
Transient killer whales, fishing nets and lines, pollution, ship strikes
YEARS I LIVE:
16–20 years

Did You See Me? Tell Your Story! _____

_____

_____

DID YOU KNOW? Both Sheila Dall sheep and I are named for William Dall, an American zoologist. He was in Alaska during the 1870s and was the first person to say he had seen us. That's why we were given his name.

Harbor Porpoise

mangaqcuar in Yupik • Phocoena phocoena

Um, hello. I'm Porter Porpoise, the smallest cetacean (si-TAY-shen) living in the waters surrounding North America. And please be very quiet or you will scare me away. I'm extremely shy and timid, so I spend most of my time by myself, cruising slowly through harbors, river estuaries (ES-tyoo-airees), bays, fjords (FEE-ords), and along the rugged coastline. Once in a while, I share meals with others of my kind when I come upon them eating an enticing school of fish, but I'm a solitary guy most of the time.

I wouldn't think of bow-riding or wake-jumping like my cousin Polly Porpoise. No way! I don't like boats or ships at all, and I dive immediately when I hear a motor. Even when I'm two hundred feet underwater, my sensitive hearing picks up those noisy boats. I stay down there for three or four minutes, if necessary, swimming as far away as possible, but then I must return to the surface to breathe. You won't see me make a big splash like my cousin Polly, though. I swim up quietly, and then arc slowly over the top of the water to allow my blowhole to break the surface. The nostrils in my blowhole open to take in the fresh air, then close again as I glide smoothly back under the water.

Now, if you're close enough when I'm breathing, you might hear sounds like a pig huffing and puffing, or someone blasting out a high, squeaky sneeze. I was nicknamed "sea pig" because of this noisy breathing. And truthfully, I do make a pig of myself sometimes when I eat, which creates a serious problem. My flat, spade-shaped teeth help me grab and bite squid, octopi, fish, or whatever else I catch, but I'm unable to chew my food. I swallow it whole, and my throat is too small to swallow anything longer than about ten inches. If I do eat something larger, it becomes stuck in my throat. That means I could choke to death! So, I look for small food to match my small throat. I also have a small, rounded head with a blunt snout, a small, curved fluke, or tail, and small, rounded flippers. Everything about me is small! So if you wave a small wave, I'll probably nod a small nod to let you know that I saw you.

My Facts

SIZE:
Cow: body, 5–6 feet long; weight, 120–130 pounds
Bull: slightly smaller than cow
COLOR:
Back: black, dark gray, or brown
Sides: pinkish-gray
Belly: white
FOOD:
Carnivorous: schooling fish including cod, whiting, pollock, herring, sardines, as well as squid and octopi
DANGERS:
Transient killer whales, sharks, fishing nets and lines, pollution, ship strikes
YEARS I LIVE:
8–12 years

Did You See Me? Tell Your Story! _____

_____

_____

DID YOU KNOW? My body looks like my cousin Polly's, but my colors are less striking. I have a black back with pinkish-gray sides and a white belly. Look for the dark line from my mouth to my flippers. That part is striking!

Steller Sea Lion

wiinaq in Sugpiaq • Eumetopias jubatus

Sampson Steller Sea Lion here, largest of the eared fur seals and sea lions. I have tiny ear flaps on each side of my head, but nothing else about me is small, especially my ROAR! I sound just like a lion in the jungle, and like that lion, I have long whiskers on my muzzle and hair around my neck that looks like a small mane. That makes me the lion of the sea, very strong and aggressive, especially when another male comes into my territory. I roar loudly to scare him away, but if he moves closer, I fight furiously to protect my part of the coast as well as my herd of cows. Whether we are in the coastal waters, or hauled out to rest on a rocky shore or an isolated island, I'm fiercely protective.

On land, I am surprisingly agile, climbing easily up rocky slopes and cliff faces to ledges, or level areas, far above the water. My front and back flippers are about the same length, and when I rotate my hind flippers beneath my body, they flatten out like feet. I walk so well on all four flippers that I could out-run you if we raced.

When I'm swimming and diving, my flippers are equally helpful. My front flippers pull me through the water with help from the strong muscles in my thick neck and massive shoulders. My hind flippers are the rudders that steer my torpedo-shaped body. Even the thick layer of blubber, or fat, right under my skin helps me swim. Blubber is lighter than water, so this fat layer helps me float. Of course my blubber is the insulation (in-soo-LAY-shun) keeping me warm in the icy, cold water. I would freeze without it, which would be awful!

You see, I am an endangered species. Our population has been declining since the mid-1970s, and no one knows exactly why. We are protected from hunters, but humans may still be the problem. The word on the waves is that pollution contributes to our decline, and that some of our food is caught in fishing nets. Or there may be dangerous parasites in the water. Who knows? But over seventy percent of all sea lions live in Alaska's waters, so watch carefully, listen for my voice, and you might see me. Wave, and I will ROOAAARRRR back at you!!!

My Facts

SIZE:
Bull: body, 10–12 feet long; weight, 2,000 pounds
Cow: body, 7–9 feet long; weight, 600–800 pounds
COLOR:
Body: light to medium brown, appearing blond when wet
Belly, flippers: yellow or orange-brown
FOOD:
Carnivorous: fish including pollock, cod, rockfish, salmon, and halibut, as well as octopi, shrimp, clams, crab
DANGERS:
Transient killer whales, fishing nets and lines, pollution, ship strikes
YEARS I LIVE:
Bull: 12–16 years
Cow: 30 years or more

Did You See Me? Tell Your Story! _____

_____

_____

_____

DID YOU KNOW? I roar loudly, but if you hear our cows, you might think you are hearing barking dogs. And our pups sound like little lambs with their quiet bleating. It is terribly confusing if we all talk at the same time.

Bearded Seal

maklag in Yupik • Erignathus barbatus

Hello. I'm Sebastian Seal, the largest of all the arctic (ARC-tic) ice seals, and I have a serious problem. I don't have a beard, and I'm called a bearded seal. I do have a mustache (MUS-tash) made of very long, flattened bristles, or whiskers, that grow on each side of my muzzle. These whiskers hang down below my chin, so it looks like I have a beard. I think it's more accurate to call me a mustached seal, don't you?

Whatever I'm called, I am one very large seal. My long, chubby body is covered with short hair, and I have a thick layer of blubber, or fat, under my skin. This blubber is what keeps me warm in the cold water since I don't have fur. My head is small for my body size, and if you are close enough to see my mouth, I look toothless. Crunchy food wore my small teeth down to stubs by the time I was nine years old. I'm fifteen now, so these teeth are hard to see.

But my claws are obvious. They are strong and sharp, and stick out from my wide, square, front flippers. These claws help me dig a hole through the ice when I'm underwater and need a way to the surface. Once I'm back on top of the ice, though, I don't bother to keep the hole open, for when I've hauled out to rest and to sleep,

I lie near the edge of the ice with my head pointed down toward the water. This way I am ready to make a quick dive if I need to escape Bella Polar Bear or a Native hunter.

When I dive, I don't go under very far. I live in shallow water, no more than two hundred feet deep, because the crabs, shrimp, and other crustaceans I eat live on the bottom of the sea. The closer I live to the bottom, the closer I am to my food. I will dive as deep as six hundred feet if I have to, but I prefer the shallows. And when I am underwater, I sing. I mean I really sing! I have a beautiful song going up and down the scale, broadcasting long trills by changing from one note to another very quickly, then ending with a long moan. No one else sings exactly the way I do, either. So listen for MY song, and hum along if you hear me!

My Facts

SIZE:
Bull: body, 8–10 feet long; weight, 600–875 pounds, more in winter
Cow: usually smaller than bull
COLOR:
Body: varied, including silver-gray, brown, and yellowish
Back: darker
FOOD:
Carnivorous: crab, shrimp, clams, worms, octopi, bottom fish, cod
DANGERS:
Polar bears, transient killer whales, walruses, Alaska Native hunters, fishing nets and lines, pollution, ship strikes
YEARS I LIVE:
25–30 years

Did You See Me? Tell Your Story! _____

_____

_____

_____

DID YOU KNOW? Some Alaska Natives hunt bearded seals for their hides and meat. The hides are used for the bottoms of boats and for harpoon lines. The meat is an important food source for subsistence (sub-SIS-tence) living.

Harbor Seal

kaeygg'yux in Ahtna • Phoca vitulina

Oh, hi! I'm Sally Harbor Seal, also called the common seal because I'm seen more often than any other pinniped (PIN-ne-ped), a marine mammal with four flippers. See me on this ice floe where I hauled out to bask in the sun? I spend about half my time out of the water, but the ice isn't the only place I rest and chill out. You will find me on sandy beaches and rocky shorelines all along coastal waters, either with a small group or a herd of thousands.

When the salmon are running up the rivers to spawn, you'll see the largest gatherings of us at the mouth of a river, waiting on the beach for the tide to come in. Salmon swim into the rivers on incoming tides, so we wait there, ready to dive in and feast!

And to be honest, I feel safer in the water catching fish than I do on land. My front and hind flippers are too short to lift my big belly and body off the ground, so I don't walk at all. Instead, I move like a plump caterpillar, undulating (UN-dyo-lay-ting) up and down like the waves of the ocean. I'm so nervous on land that I dive into the water immediately if you or any other land creature moves in my direction. And if you come too close and frighten me, I grunt loudly at you as I slip into the water.

The water is my world, where I leave everyone else behind, and swim and dive alone. Normally, I cruise about five miles per hour, but when I'm chasing dinner, my hind flippers with their webbed toes move from side-to-side so fast that I zoom through the water at ten or twelve miles per hour. These flippers help me dive as deep as fourteen hundred feet into the darkness, too, where I might stay as long as half an hour. When I am underwater for that long, my body temperature drops very low, my heart beats much more slowly, and my lungs deflate, or push out all air. My ears and nose have membranes (MEM-branes) that close to keep the water out, and my eyes have an extra, clear eyelid for protection. I'm built for the water, and I love it! So look for a swimming fool in fjords, rivers, harbors, bays, and along the coastline. I'm everywhere!

My Facts

SIZE:
Bull: body, 5–6 feet long; weight, 200–250 pounds
Cow: 25 percent smaller than bull
COLOR:
Varied: see "Did You Know?"
FOOD:
Carnivorous: all kinds of fish, shellfish, squid, octopi
DANGERS:
Transient killer whales, sea lions, polar bears, wolves, fishing nets and gear, ship strikes
YEARS I LIVE:
Bull: 20 years
Cow: 30 years

Did You See Me? Tell Your Story! _____
_____
_____
_____

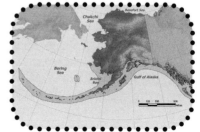

DID YOU KNOW? Our color varies greatly. Some of us are dark with light spots, others are light with dark spots, and still others are solid silver-gray to dark brown. Just remember: I'll be alone in the water but with a group on land.

Northern Fur Seal

aataak in Alutiiq • Callorhinus ursinus

Hello. I'm Stanley, a Northern fur seal, or the Alaska fur seal. I am here with some of my harem (HAIR-em), or group of cows, and their pups on one of the Pribilof Islands in the Bering Sea. We are about three hundred miles west of mainland Alaska, where almost sixty-five percent of all fur seal pups are born every summer. I returned to this rocky beach in May with thousands of other bulls and established my rookery, the place where my cows have their pups. The cows arrived between mid-June and early July, just in time to give birth.

The pups are all doing well now, and I've been pup-sitting the youngsters in their playpen, or "puppy pod," where they play and sleep. I began guarding them when they were just a few days old so their moms could leave to feed on fish and squid. After eating for a few days, the moms returned, and each one was able to find her own pup. She would call to it, listen to the voices that answered, and then move close enough to recognize the unique smell of her own offspring. The cows have continued to leave for longer and longer periods of time. And in October, just a few weeks away, they will leave permanently to spend the winter in the warm Pacific waters between Southern California and Japan. When they leave, the pups panic at first and scatter in all directions, but eventually they find their way to the warmer southern waters, also.

I stay here, roaming around the cold ocean, eating at night when the fish come closer to the surface, sleeping on the water curled up on my back, and simply living. I'm safe here, but it wasn't always that way. You see, our fur is incredibly soft, luxurious, and thick, with more than three hundred twenty thousand hairs on every square inch of our bodies. (You have one hundred thousand hairs on your whole head!) This fur created serious problems for my ancestors in the late 1700s. Russian whale hunters realized they could make lots of money if they killed us and then sold our fur. They were joined by hunters from the United States and other countries, and millions of us were destroyed. We were hunted almost to extinction until laws were written in 1911, making it illegal to hunt us. I'm safe now, so I would love to see you! I know you won't harm me!

My Facts

SIZE:
Bull: body, 6 feet long; weight, 300–600 pounds
Cow: body, 4 feet long; weight, 75–100 pounds
COLOR:
Back: gray, brown, brownish-black
Throat, chest: lighter
Mane: light-colored (on bull only)
Pup: black
FOOD:
Carnivorous: schooling fish including herring, smelt, sole, flounder, saury, shrimp, squid
DANGERS:
Transient killer whales, Stellar sea lions, fishing nets and lines, pollution, ship strikes
YEARS I LIVE:
26–30 years

Did You See Me? Tell Your Story! _____

_____

_____

_____

DID YOU KNOW? My thick fur does not grow on my flippers, which are just bare skin. When I am too warm under my heavy coat, I float on my back and move my flippers in the air. It looks like I am greeting you with a wave!

Ringed Seal

nayir in Yupik • Phoca hispida

Hello! I'm Sakura Ringed Seal, smallest of the light-colored northern seals and most numerous of all Alaska's seals. I look like Sally Harbor Seal except I have rings all over my back. (That's why I'm called a ringed seal.) I'm resting on the ice after my half-hour fishing trip in the cold Arctic water. I relax on the "fast" ice, ice fastened (fas-end) or attached to the shoreline, during the winter. But it is summertime now, so I am away from land on the pack ice, a huge mass of ice made up of large, individual chunks packed together.

I swim and fish under the pack ice, but I have to be careful. If I don't find a break or opening, I could become trapped underneath, unable to swim to the surface to breathe. But don't worry. I have incredibly strong claws on my front flippers, especially the long, sharp, pointed first claw. These claws are strong enough for me to dig my own cone-shaped breathing holes through ice as thick as six feet. Once I have a hole opened to the surface, I keep it clear by continuing to scrape the ice away as it forms. And every year, near one of these holes, I build a denning lair where I give birth to my pup.

This lair, made of snow, is about six feet wide and nine feet long, and it becomes larger as I add more chambers and tunnels. My pup lives in this lair for at least two months, gaining strength and growing while its white birth-coat changes to adult colors. When my pup is strong enough, it slips through the nearby breathing hole and swims away to live on its own.

My denning lair isn't my only snow structure. I build snow caves over some of my other breathing holes, and I swim straight up into these caves to avoid bad weather and to hide from dangerous Bella Polar Bear. I am her favorite food, and she'll do anything to catch me! When she doesn't grab me on top of the ice, she waits next to one of my snow caves until I come to the surface, then crashes through the snow to snatch me. She watches for me everywhere, and if I'm not alert, I become her dinner. So please, warn me if you see Bella!

My Facts

SIZE:
Bull: body, up to 4 feet long; weight, 140–190 pounds
Cow: slightly smaller than bull
COLOR:
Back, sides: gray with black spots ringed with white
Belly: buff or cream
FOOD:
Carnivorous: small fish including arctic and saffron cod, herring, shrimp, crustaceans, zooplankton
DANGERS:
Polar bears, arctic foxes, walruses, transient killer whales, wolves, wolverines, Alaska Native hunters, pollution, ship strikes
YEARS I LIVE:
25–40 years

Did You See Me? Tell Your Story! _____

_____

_____

_____

DID YOU KNOW? I am called a "true seal," or "earless seal." I'm called earless because I do not have visible outer ear flaps, but I do have ears and hear perfectly. As a true seal, I have four flippers and cannot "walk" on land.

Pacific Walrus

wiinarpak in Sugpiaq • *Odobenus rosmarus*

Oh, hello. I'm Walter Walrus, and I'm having trouble with Waldo. He wandered into my territory, and when bulls like us meet, we lift our heads, then turn sideways to inspect each other's tusks. Whoever has the biggest tusks is dominant (DOM-in-ant), or the boss, and the other bull leaves. But Waldo won't go away and has challenged me to fight, even though my tusks are obviously longer and larger. Now our inch-thick hides will have new bruises and stab wounds from jabbing each other with our strong tusks. That darn Waldo!

Say, did you know that tusks are actually canine (CAY-nine) teeth grown very long? Our cows have them, too, but we bulls have longer, thicker, straighter ones. My tusks are about thirty-five inches long and weigh ten pounds, and they will continue to grow my whole life. I use these teeth for more than just fighting. When I haul myself out of the water to rest on the rocks or ice, I push myself forward with my strong hind flippers, then use my tusks like arms to lift myself up. In the wintertime, when ice has formed on top of the water, my tusks gently chip it away, making a hole large enough for me to slide through into the water. I enter the water headfirst, but I land on my side or back to keep from breaking a tusk. And once I'm in the water, I usually dive no more than three hundred feet deep.

The clams, worms, crabs, and other tasty morsels I eat live in the ocean's muddy floor, so I stay in shallow water to be closer to the bottom. I use the hundreds of stiff bristles on my broad muzzle to help me find food in the mud, then I open my thick lips, pull my victim into my mouth with my strong tongue, crack its shell with my powerful jaws and teeth, and draw out the tasty meat. I spend part of my day eating, and the rest of the time I haul out on rocky areas to relax.

Whether I'm on land or underwater, I'm a loud singer. Huge sacs in my neck help me make a deep bellow that sounds like church bells. So follow the church bells near the ocean, then look for a large pinniped (PIN-a-ped) with scars all over its wrinkly, bumpy neck and shoulders. Find me, and I will sing for you!

My Facts

SIZE:
Bull: body, 10–12 feet long; weight, 4,000 pounds
Cow: body, 8–9 feet long; weight, 2,000 pounds
COLOR:
Body: cinnamon to rusty-brown
FOOD:
Carnivorous: clams, mussels, shrimp, worms, crab, sea cucumbers, seals, seabirds
DANGERS:
Transient killer whales, polar bears, Alaska Native hunters, pollution, ship strikes
YEARS I LIVE:
30–40 years

Did You See Me? Tell Your Story! _____
_____
_____

DID YOU KNOW? Watch me on live webcam from Round Island, about four hundred miles southwest of Anchorage. Go to http://explore.org/live-cams/player/walrus-cam-round-island to see me in real, live action!

Beluga Whale

telaani in Ahtna • Delphinapterus leucas

Oh, hello! I'm Wilma Whale, a small toothed whale, here with my baby beluga (ba-LOO-ga) BamBam. We are the only white whales in the world, but if you notice, BamBam isn't white yet. She was born a dark, gray-brown color, and her skin is slowly becoming lighter. It will be six years before she is completely white.

Did you notice how shiny, clean, and white I am right now? My skin becomes dirty and yellowish throughout the year, so every summer I molt, or shed, my old skin. Some of it falls off naturally, but most of it is scraped off by gravel and rough sand on the bottom of the shallow waters where I swim. I may be in coastal waters, inlets, bays, estuaries (ES-tyoo-air-ees), or chasing spawning salmon far up the rivers. Wherever I am, I swim upside-down, on my side, *or* right-side-up, so it's easy to rub off all that dirty skin. And I'm able to see where I am going because I bend my neck from side to side to look around. No other whale does that!

Know what else is different about me? I have no dorsal fin on my back! I have smooth ridges, but that is all. Also, my head is small with a bulbous (BUL-bus) forehead that looks like a little watermelon grew inside. That's my echolocation (EK-o-lo-CAY-shun) chamber. I make many loud, clicking sounds that strike fish or other surfaces, which causes an echo to come back to me. That echo passes through my melon-like chamber to "tell" me where an object is located. I find my food, as well as obstacles, in the underwater darkness this way. And in the winter, when I swim under the ice, echolocation helps me find breaks in the ice, through which I come up for air.

When there is no ice, I may twitter and roll as I surface to breathe, or I might "snorkel," which means only my blowhole breaks the surface. My pod of ten to several hundred all breathe at the same time, so watch for us. We won't stay above water long, since we come up for a quick breath before diving under for another ten or fifteen minutes. And look! My pod just went under, probably chasing salmon toward that river. We have to go! Wave if you see us!

My Facts

SIZE:
Bull: body, 11–16 feet long; weight, 3,300 pounds
Cow: body, 9–12 feet long; weight, 3,000 pounds
COLOR:
Body: white
Calf: dark gray, lightening to white over time
FOOD:
Carnivorous: squid, octopi, shrimp, crab, clams, mussels; fish including herring, cod, flatfish, salmon, lingcod
DANGERS:
Transient killer whales, polar bears, fishing gear and nets, entrapment under sea ice, pollution, ship strikes
YEARS I LIVE:
30–35 years

Did You See Me? Tell Your Story! _____

_____

_____

DID YOU KNOW? My nickname is "sea canary" because I sing and make more sounds than any other marine mammal. I chirp, whistle, click, mew, squeal and grunt. The sounds help me echolocate (EK-o-LO-kate) as well as "talk" with other belugas.

Blue Whale

ar'uq in Alutiiq • Balaenoptera musculus

Salutations. I'm Wagner Blue Whale, the largest animal that has ever lived on Earth. That means I am larger than all extinct dinosaurs, elephants, other whales, and anyone else. Some of my ancestors were one hundred feet long and weighed three hundred tons. Today we are smaller, but I am still massive at eighty-five feet long and weighing one hundred and fifty tons. That is the length of three school buses lined up end to end, and the weight of more than eleven buses. My heart is the size of a small car. An adult elephant could stand on the bottom of my closed mouth and not touch the top, and my tongue weighs more than that same elephant! Now do you understand how enormous I am?

My long body is slender, though, and I have a flat head that is U-shaped in front. And from my lower jaw back toward my tummy are more than seventy pleats that balloon out to hold the huge amount of water I swallow when I eat. I gulp in the water, then partially close my mouth, tighten my throat muscles, and force the water back out across my baleen (bay-LEEN). This baleen looks like three-foot-long strands of fur, and it hangs from more than three hundred fifty black plates in the top of my mouth. As the water rushes out of my mouth, millions of krill, or tiny crustaceans (crus-TAY-shuns), become caught in this baleen. Then, all I have to do is swipe my tongue across it to remove the krill and to swallow them. Yum!

I need to eat about four tons of krill every day, and to catch this much, I swim near the surface of the water looking for dense swarms of these tiny creatures. I cruise along at about thirteen miles per hour, gulping water and eating when I find the food.

I don't breach, or do anything fancy when I come up out of the water, but I do have the tallest spout, or blow, of all the whales in the ocean. When I blow my strongest, I will shoot a narrow stream of water thirty feet high for five seconds or more. And when I shoot my mouth off and "talk," I make the loudest, most booming moans, trills, and clicks that can be heard over seven hundred miles away! Speaking of talk, I need to stop chatting now and eat! I'm hungry. Yell if you see me!

My Facts

SIZE:
Cow: body, 75–90 feet long; weight, 110–150 tons
Bull: slightly smaller than cow
COLOR:
Body: blue-gray with lighter gray mottling (spots)
Underside of flukes, flippers, belly: whitish
FOOD:
Carnivorous: krill
DANGERS:
Transient killer whales, fishing nets and lines, pollution, ship strikes
YEARS I LIVE:
80–90 years

Did You See Me? Tell Your Story! _____

_____

_____

DID YOU KNOW? Long ago, there were over three hundred fifty thousand of us. We were hunted by whalers in the early twentieth century and almost none of us survived. Protected now, three to four thousand of us live north of the Equator.

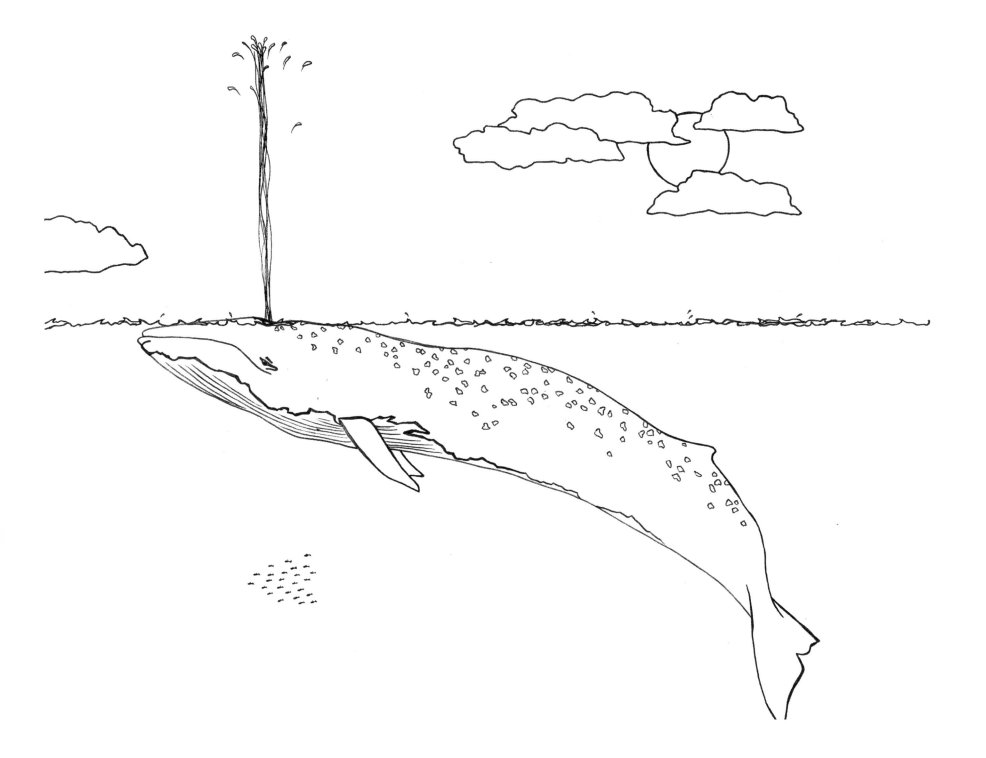

Bowhead Whale

arveq in Yu'pik • Balaena mysticetus

Hello! I'm Wanda Bowhead Whale, the whale with the great, big, upside down smile. See how my mouth and jaw arch from the front of my head all the way back to my eye? This curve looks like the bow people use when they shoot arrows, and that is why I'm called a bowhead whale.

I have the largest head of any animal in the entire animal kingdom, taking up almost one-third of my entire body length. This huge head has saved my life more than once. You see, I live farther north than any other whale, staying near or under the pack ice all year long. Sometimes, when I'm under the ice, there are no openings for me to come to the surface for air. That's when I use my enormous head, breaking through ice as thick as three feet, opening my own way to the surface, where I breathe through the two blowholes on the top of my head.

Often I eat when I come up for air, too. My food lives at all levels of the ocean, but near the top I find massive swarms of zooplankton (ZOO-uh-PLANK-ton), or tiny shrimp-like animals. I swim into the middle of the mass, swallow gallons of water containing the zooplankton, then push the water back out of my mouth to trap the food in my baleen. And by the way, my mouth is large enough inside for a polar bear to stand straight up with room to stretch!

Did you notice the baleen in the drawing of me? My baleen is the longest of any whale, hanging down thirteen feet from at least seven hundred dark gray plates in my upper jaw. It traps tons of food for me, which I need for maintaining my large, rotund body and two-foot-thick blubber. Blubber, my fat layer, is like a big blanket insulating me in this icy cold water, and it stores important vitamins and nutrients to help me stay healthy.

But my blubber created a problem. People want the nutrients and valuable oil it contains, and my ancestors were hunted until they were almost all killed. We are safe now, because the laws say that only Alaska Natives are allowed to hunt us as part of their subsistence (sub-SIS-tense) lifestyle. And if your lifestyle allows, visit the icepack in the far north. I'll show you my marvelous smile!

My Facts

SIZE:
Cow: body, 45–60 feet long; weight, 70–100 tons
Bull: slightly smaller than cow
COLOR:
Back, sides: dark blue or black
Belly, chin: white patches or spots
Tail: light band in front of fluke
FOOD:
Carnivorous: zooplankton, krill, copepods, other invertebrates
DANGERS:
Alaska Native hunters, transient killer whales, fishing nets and lines, pollution, ship strikes
YEARS I LIVE:
150–200 years (longest living mammal)

Did You See Me? Tell Your Story! _____

_____

_____

_____

DID YOU KNOW? I love to sing and make sounds. My long songs cover seven octaves with very complicated patterns that I repeat over and over. When I roam these waters with my relatives, we sing to each other for days at a time.

Fin Whale

yaay in Lingít • Balaenoptera physalus

Wilbur's the name, Wilbur Fin Whale, the second largest mammal in the ocean. Only Wagner Blue Whale is bigger than I am. I may be huge, but I need your help. I want a name other than boring "fin" whale. I was given this name because of the two-foot-tall dorsal fin low on my back that looks like a shark's fin. Like that creature's fin, mine has the same backward arch, sharp turn at the top, and inside curving hook-shape on its back edge. My fin is closer to my flukes than to my blowhole and is very easy to see when I surface.

I also have another name that's a little more interesting: Razorback. This one came from the noticeable ridge down my back that runs from my dorsal fin to my flukes. I guess someone thought it looked sharp as a razor, so I was awarded the nickname.

The thing is, though, I have other features that are much more distinctive than either my fin or my ridge. My long, sleek body is dark gray except for the white on my belly. But under my flat head, with its cool V-shaped nose, the sides of my lower jaw and baleen are different colors! The right side of my lower lip and the front of my baleen are yellowish white, but on the left side, these parts are dark gray. My coloring is asymmetrical (a-sim-MET-ri-cul), meaning the two sides have colors that don't match at all! Pretty neat, huh?

Plus, I have light gray chevrons, or V patterns, above each flipper that point toward my eyes. These markings really stand out! When I'm swimming by, you will notice my markings and unique coloring before you ever see my fin or razorback.

And I will be swimming fast because I am one of the speediest swimmers of all the great whales. I move anywhere from sixteen to twenty-two miles per hour, and when I decide to dive, you will know it. I blow four or five times, and shoot a narrow column of water fifteen or twenty feet into the air. Then I make a loud, whistling sound, as I go under without showing you my fluke. I may go as deep as a thousand feet and stay under for fifteen minutes.

So, while I'm under, will you try to think of a better name for me? Maybe Chevy, or Symi? I need your help!

My Facts

SIZE:
Cow: body, up to 80 feet long; weight, 50–80 tons
Bull: slightly smaller than cow
COLOR:
Body: dark gray, black
Belly: lighter
On back above flippers: light V marking
Lower jaw: irregular coloring
FOOD:
Carnivorous: zooplankton, krill, anchovies, herring, other schooling fish, squid
DANGERS:
Transient killer whales, fishing nets and lines, pollution, ship strikes
YEARS I LIVE:
80–100 years

Did You See Me? Tell Your Story! _____

_____

_____

_____

DID YOU KNOW? I live in cool, polar waters in the summertime. There, I eat up to two tons of food a day. In the winter, I swim south to warmer tropical water. In both areas, I stay far from shore in the deepest part of the ocean.

Gray Whale

Ar'uq in Sugpiaq • *Eschrichtius robustus*

Think I'm eating mud? Hi, I'm Willard Gray Whale, and I am actually having lunch now that I'm back in my summertime home in the Bering Sea. I eat little creatures living in the muddy ocean floor by swallowing big gulps of water and mud, then pushing the gooey stuff back out through my mouth. The delicious worms, plankton (PLANK-tun), and other tasty morsels are caught in my extremely coarse baleen. I say "coarse" because my baleen is like a thick, stiff brush with at least twenty short bristles per inch. These bristles become loaded with the small invertebrates (in-VER-ta-brayts), so all I have to do is scrape them off with my tongue and swallow.

I stay down here as long as half an hour, eating as much as possible because I'm very hungry right now. I just returned from spending the winter in the warm waters off of Baja California, and I don't eat anything when I'm there. I also don't eat while I'm swimming along the Pacific Coast, traveling five thousand miles in each direction on my long journey. I lose at least twelve thousand pounds, so once I return to this cold northern ocean, I consume at least one ton of food every day. I have to gain back my weight and rebuild the reserves of fat I lost.

I come to the surface to breathe, and when I do, watch for me to breach. That means I leap partway out of the water, then make a huge splash as I land on my side. Breaching is a way for me to knock off some of the ugly barnacles (BAR-na-kuls) and creepy whale lice that live on my body, especially on my narrow, pointed head. Barnacles are hard-shelled, living creatures that attach themselves to many objects in the ocean, including me. Thousands of white barnacles grow in clusters on my skin, more than on any other whale. The barnacles don't hurt me, but they make a perfect place for the orange whale lice to live. Lice do harm me by eating my skin and damaging my tissues. Yuck! I'll never knock them all off, but I sure do keep trying.

And just to let you know, I'm the whale people ride out to see on those whale-watching boats. That might be the way for you to find me. Wave and holler if you see me!

My Facts

SIZE:
Cow: body, 45–50 feet long; weight, 30–40 tons
Bull: slightly smaller than cow
COLOR:
Body: dark gray with white splotches
Face, head: splotches of white barnacles
FOOD:
Carnivorous: small crustaceans, plankton, mollusks, worms
DANGERS:
Transient killer whales, fishing nets and
lines, pollution, ship strikes
YEARS I LIVE:
40–60 years

Did You See Me? Tell Your Story! _____

_____

_____

DID YOU KNOW? I have no dorsal fin, but I have a definite hump and numerous bumps leading to my tail stock. Below my tail stock is my fluke, which is at least twelve feet across with a deep notch in the center. You'll see it when I dive.

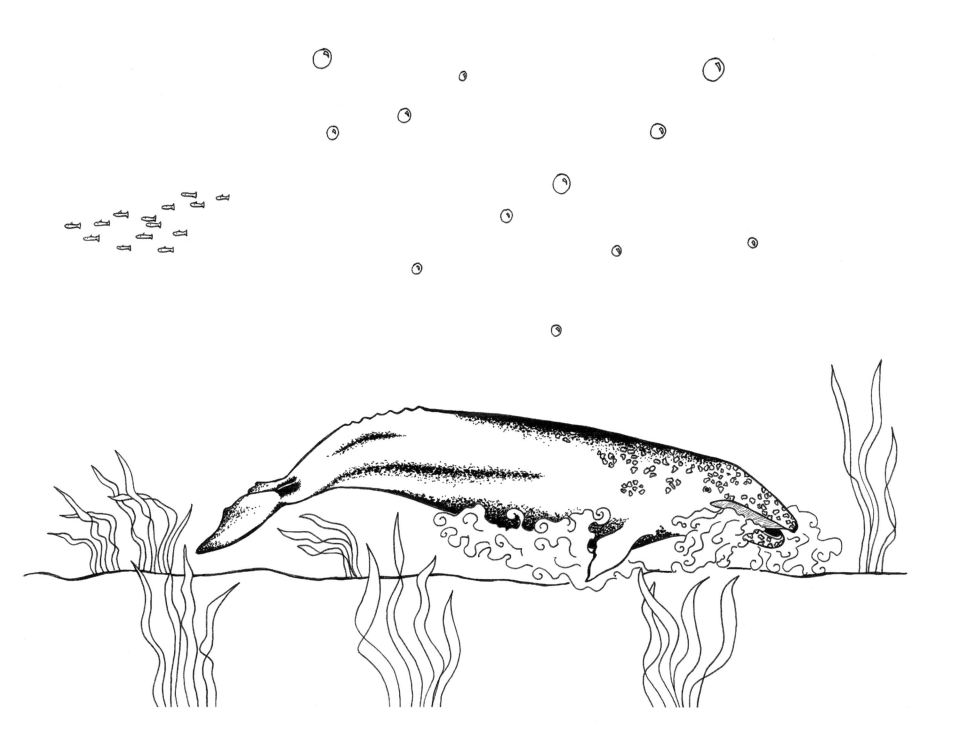

Humpback Whale

arwer in Yupik • Megaptera novaeangliae

Why, hello. I'm Willamae Humpback Whale, and I'm the whale you are most likely to see. I "play" on the water's surface more than any other whale. I breach, leaping completely out of the water, then fall on my back or side making a huge splash. I spyhop, standing straight up in the water to look all around. Sometimes I show off my unique flippers, which are the longest flippers of any great whale, by floating on the surface, then whacking my flipper on the water to create a great splash. While I'm slapping the water, you might see the tubercles (TOO-ber-kuls), or large bumps, all along the front edges of the flippers. I also love to lobtail, or slap the water with my huge fluke. I lift my tail high out of the water, crash it back down on the surface, and then dive to see if I stunned any krill or little schools of fish. A stunned fish won't move a fin, giving me an incredibly easy meal.

I eat more than a ton of food a day, and lobtailing is just one of the sneaky techniques I use to trap my prey. I look for "bait balls," or big, round clusters of tiny fish swimming together in a tight school. I swim directly into the fish with my mouth wide open, inhaling millions of them in one bite. But the best way for me to consume massive amounts of food is to bubble-net with other humpbacks. We swim in a circle below a school of fish or krill, blowing air bubbles to create a curtain of bubbles as we move the fish closer together and up toward the surface. Then we swoop straight up through the mass of fish, mouths open, and take in huge amounts of water and fish. The pleats on my chest expand to hold the water until I push it back out through my dark baleen, trapping tons of food.

I eat . . . Oh, no! There's old Wallace singing again. We cows don't sing at all, but our bulls have more sounds and sing longer than any animal in the world. They grunt, moan, shriek, whoop, and wail, changing tones all the time. Supposedly, they sing to attract me or to show who's boss. Scientists don't know for sure, and I don't either. But listen for their noises, watch for my splash, and wave if you see me playing!

My Facts

SIZE:
Cow: body, 52–58 feet long; weight, 35–44 tons
Bull: slightly smaller than cow
COLOR:
Back, sides: dark gray to black
Belly, throat, fluke, flippers: varied amounts of white and spotting
FOOD:
Carnivorous: krill, and schooling fish like herring, capelin and sand lance
DANGERS:
Transient killer whales, fishing nets and lines, pollution, ship strikes
YEARS I LIVE:
40–50 years or more

Did You See Me? Tell Your Story! _____

_____

_____

_____

DID YOU KNOW? I was named "humpback" because of the short, stocky dorsal fin on my back that looks like a hump. The shape of this hump, and the differences in the length, shape, and knobs on my flippers, let scientists identify each one of us.

Killer Whale

arlluk in Alutiiq • Orcinus orca

I am Warrick KILLER Whale, a transient (TRAN-see-ent) killer whale and the deadliest of all whales. Transient means I do not stay in one place very long. Instead, I roam continually along the coast and out into the ocean. I hunt as I wander, killing and eating any marine mammal I find. Seals, porpoises, sea lions, dolphins, small whales, polar bears . . . Everyone is on MY menu. I even leap up on rocks or slither onto beaches to drag marine *or* land mammals into the water for my meal.

I'm known as the wolf of the sea, hunting with a pack or pod when I want to kill larger prey, just like wolves do on land. A group of five or six of us circle our victim, move in closer and closer, then charge once it is trapped. Some of us bite with our sharp, cone-shaped teeth to make it bleed, and others slap the victim with our tail flukes to stun it. We force the creature underwater until it drowns, then drag its dead body back to the surface to eat. We trap and kill even the biggest whales when we work together this way!

But I must tell you not all killer whales behave as I do. There are two other populations, or types, of killer whales who are not dangerous at all. Resident killer whales live in pods of ten to thirty, usually a cow and her offspring, with different pods staying in their own part of the ocean. They don't wander like me, and they only eat fish such as salmon. Borrr-ing! The other population, the offshore group, is just as simple in their tastes. They dine on fish and sharks, never eating delicious mammals. These big groupies, with pods of fifty, seventy-five, or even a hundred, live at least ten miles from shore most of the time. I don't hang out with these other populations, and they stay away from me, too. We don't even talk to each other because the whistles, screams, and squeaks we all use to echolocate (EK-o-LO-kate) and communicate are only understood by our own pod. The populations even look a bit different. My dorsal fin is tall and pointed, while all the others have rounder, shorter fins.

So look for a pod of whales with tall, black dorsal fins moving together close to shore. We're the real killer whales. I won't eat YOU, but stay out of my waters, anyway. Got it?

My Facts

SIZE:
Bull: body, 27–32 feet long; weight, 9–11 tons
Cow: body, 23–28 feet long; weight, 5–7 tons
COLOR:
Body: black
Belly, chin: white
Sides, near eyes: white patches
Dorsal fin: black with white "saddle" behind it
FOOD:
Depends on population
DANGERS:
Pollution, capture for display in aquariums, ship strikes
YEARS I LIVE:
Bull: 30–50 years
Cow: 50–80 years

Did You See Me? Tell Your Story! _____

_____

_____

_____

DID YOU KNOW? We are the largest member of the dolphin family, but we are called whales due to our large size. We live all over the world, in all parts of all oceans. No other mammal lives in as many places in the world as we do.

Minke Whale

telaani in Ahtna • Balaenoptera acutorostrata

Greetings! My name is Wilhelmina Minke Whale. That is pronounced WILL-hel-MEE-na MING-key. (You know how to pronounce "whale!") I'm the smallest of all the baleen whales in the Northern Hemisphere (HEM-i-sfear), and too small to bother anyone. I'm not social, so I stay by myself most of the time. I join a herd of my kind to eat if I'm hungry, and there is a giant school of cod or herring to share. When I'm full, though, I leave to be alone again.

Sometimes I head out to the open ocean, and other times I wander along the coastline, into shallow bays or inlets. Wherever I swim, I'm always on the lookout for boats. You see, I am extremely curious about boats and swim right up to one, especially if it isn't moving. I cruise underwater until I am close to a vessel, then quietly break the surface, snout or nose first, and come up to see what's happening. And when my curiosity is satisfied, I arch my tail stock, roll quietly up and out of the water, and smoothly back under without raising my fluke.

Of course, there are times I leap completely out of the water so I make a big splash when I crash down. That is when you might see what I look like. I'm a dark grayish-black color, slim and streamlined, with an extremely narrow, pointed head that has a raised ridge right down the middle. There are light gray, irregular markings near my dorsal fin and on each side above my flippers. My flippers are short and pointed, and have distinctive white bands on them. Low on my back is my tall, triangular-shaped dorsal fin, with its backward hook. The top of my fin is either curved or tipped over. And this streamlined body is built for swimming. I am the fastest of all baleen whales, zooming through the water at up to twenty-eight miles per hour. Even scary old Warrick Killer Whale, the fierce, toothed whale, has a difficult time catching me.

Please, if you catch sight of me, ignore me, even if you are close enough to see the white baleen in my mouth. You know I'm shy and don't like attention. Watch me, but you'll just embarrass me if you wave.

My Facts

SIZE:
Cow: body, 28–30 feet long; weight, 8–9 tons
Bull: slightly smaller than cow
COLOR:
Body: dark gray to black
Belly, mid-flank band, flipper patches, neck chevron: white
FOOD:
Carnivorous: krill, herring, mackerel, cod
DANGERS:
Transient killer whales, fishing nets and lines, pollution, ship strikes
YEARS I LIVE:
45–50 years

Did You See Me? Tell Your Story! _____

_____

_____

_____

DID YOU KNOW? There are more of my kind than of any other whale. Because we are so small, whalers have never bothered hunting us. The big whales provided more blubber, oil, and meat, so they are the ones who were hunted.

Sperm Whale

kun kaj Gajaaw in Haida • *Physeter macrocephalus*

Hello. I'm Wilson Sperm Whale, largest of the toothed whales. I have twenty-six pairs of pointed, cone-shaped teeth on my lower jaw, and when I close my mouth, these teeth fit smoothly into holes in my upper jaw. Some of my teeth are as long as eight inches and weigh over two pounds! That's not a problem, though, since I have a massive head that is almost one-third my total body length. I'm about fifty feet long, and my head makes up almost eighteen feet of that length. And right in front, I have a completely flat, five-foot-high nose, the tallest nose of any animal. I also hold the record for the largest brain.

But there is something more incredible about my head than its size, my nose, or my brain. My head is full of a special oil called spermaceti (sperm-a-SE-tee). When the oil is in my head, it is a liquid, but when it is taken out and cooled, the liquid becomes a solid wax. The liquid oil and solid wax were both extremely valuable in the nineteenth century during the Industrial Revolution. The oil was used to lubricate (LOO-bri-cate) expensive machines, to help them run better, and it was also burned in old-fashioned oil lamps for light. The solid wax was made into candles and used in expensive cosmetics (koz-MET-iks). Whalers killed so many of my ancestors for this valuable oil that we almost became extinct! But laws were put in place to protect us, and we are not endangered anymore.

In fact, there are enough of us that you might see me. My body is wrinkled and scarred, and I have a hump instead of a dorsal fin. Behind my hump are knuckles, or bumps, all the way to my tail stump. You might see me if you look for a log lying completely still on the surface that suddenly spouts water forward and to the left. I'm "logging," and getting ready to dive more than a mile underwater. I will stay down for two hours or more! To have enough air, I must breathe at least seventy times through my blowhole, blowing a small, bushy spout of water every time I take a breath. And since I travel to warmer waters near Japan in the winter, summertime is when you will need to watch for my huge nose and head here in Alaska. Find me, and I'll "log" for you!

My Facts

SIZE:
Bull: body, at least 50 feet long; weight, 50–60 tons
Cow: body, 36 feet long; weight, 22–28 tons
COLOR:
Body: dark gray
Mouth, jaw, underside: white
FOOD:
Carnivorous: squid, octopi, sharks, rays, fish
DANGERS:
Fishing nets and lines, pollution, ship strikes
YEARS I LIVE:
60–70 years or more

Did You See Me? Tell Your Story! _____

_____

_____

_____

DID YOU KNOW? The famous, white whale Moby-Dick was a sperm whale that lived long ago. Whalers said he was a huge, violent creature who would attack and overturn whaling ships when sailors tried to harpoon him.

Glossary

abalone: a shelled animal whose shell is shaped like an ear and lined with mother-of-pearl

aquatic: having to do with animals or plants that live in water

arthropod: animal with no backbone (also called an invertebrate), whose skeleton is on the outside (also called an exoskeleton) Examples: shrimp, lobster, crab, and barnacles

baleen: large, comb-like plates hanging from the roof of some whales' mouths to catch food

barnacle: crustacean with a hard shell that attaches permanently to underwater surfaces

bow-riding: swimming near the front of a boat as it moves through the water

carnivore: animal who eats meat only

abalone

carnivorous: describes one who eats meat only

cetacean: all whales, dolphins, and porpoises (the order *Cetacea*)

circumpolar: around or near the North or South Pole

crustacean: small, insect-like creature with a hard shell or crust, such as shrimp, crab, krill, and barnacles

dorsal fin: the fin on the back of some cetaceans

fjord: a narrow, deep waterway or inlet between high cliffs formed by glaciers

flukes: the two flat, horizontal sections of the tail on a cetacean, notched where they meet

guard hairs: long, coarse outer hairs that cover soft underfur on some mammals

fjord

baleen

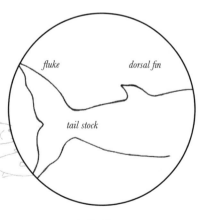

fluke   dorsal fin

tail stock

fluke

kelp

haul out: climb out of the water on land or ice

ice floe: a flat piece of floating ice

inlet: a narrow passageway of water along a coastline that goes inland

kelp: seaweed that grows in the ocean

keratin: main material in fingernails, hair, antlers, horns, baleen

krill: small crustaceans that whales eat, and that look like shrimp

notch: V-shaped point where two sections of flukes meet

plankton: tiny, drifting plants and animals in all bodies of water

spy-hop: when a cetacean "stands" straight up in the water and looks around

tail stock: the narrow, muscular part between the body and the tail flukes of a whale

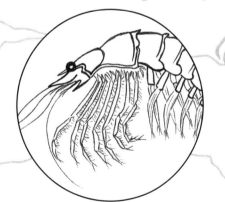

krill

spy-hop

Learn More
About the Mammals of Alaska

Places to see a variety of mammals:

Alaganik Slough Trail, Milepost 17, Copper River Highway

Alaska Sea Life Center, Seward

Alaska Wildlife Conservation Center near the Portage turnoff

Alaska Zoo, Anchorage

Chugach State Park, Eagle River/Anchorage

Denali National Park

Kenai Spur Highway and Kenai River Viewing Platforms, Soldatna/Kenai

Kincaid Park, Anchorage

Moose Pond, Lost Lake Trail

Muskox Farm, near Palmer

Potter Marsh, Anchorage

Reindeer Farm, Palmer

Richardson Highway between Paxson and Delta Junction (bison)

Sterling Highway, Milepost 106, Windy Corner turnout (Dall sheep)

Places to see bears:

McNeil River Game Sanctuary (permit only)

Katmai National Park

Russian River Falls out of Russian River Campground, Milepost 52 on Sterling Highway

Hidden Creek near Skilak Lake

Salmon Creek near Hyder

Kodiak Island

Chilkoot Lake State Park

Numerous fly-in opportunities

Online:

Alaska Department of Fish and Game website for all animals: http://www.adfg.alaska.gov/index.cfm?adfg=animals.listall

http://explore.org/live-cams/player/walrus-cam-round-island

National Oceanic and Atmospheric Administration for kids: http://oceanservice.noaa.gov/kids/

http://www.kidzone.ws/animals/mammals.htm

Further reading:

Alaska Mammals, Alaska Geographic

Alaska's Mammals, by Dave Smith and Tom Walker

Mammals of Alaska, Alaska Geographic Guides

The Nature of Alaska: A Waterford Press Field Guide

Peterson's Field Guides to Mammals of North America

Whalewatcher, by Trevor Day